Absolute Crime Presents:

Wrongfully Accused

15 People Sentenced to Prison for a Crime They Didn't Commit

**ABSO UTE
CR ME**

By William Webb

Absolute Crime Books

www.absolutecrime.com

Cover Image © i3alda - Fotolia.com

Table of Contents

About Us

Absolute Crime publishes only the best true crime literature. Our focus is on the crimes that you've probably never heard of, but you are fascinated to read more about. With each engaging and gripping story, we try to let readers relive moments in history that some people have tried to forget.

Remember, our books are not meant for the faint at heart. We don't hold back—if a crime is bloody, we let the words splatter across the page so you can experience the crime in the most horrifying way!

If you enjoy this book, please visit our homepage to see other books we offer; if you have any feedback, we'd love to hear from you!

Introduction

Wrongful accusations are among the worst miscarriages of justice because they harm the innocent while letting the guilty walk free. Unfortunately, these are far more common than most of us would like to believe.

Dozens of innocent people have been imprisoned for murders they didn't commit. In a more frightening turn of events, over 130 death row inmates in the United States were found to be wrongfully accused in the last 20 years.

Wrongfully accusations are among the worst crimes because they undermine the justice system itself. Not only do the innocent suffer and the guilty walk, but public faith in law enforcement and the courts is also undermined. Hopefully, examples such as these will inspire reforms that will make the system more effective and prevent such nightmares from occurring in the future.

Alan Gell

It's rare that a wrongfully convicted individual gets a chance to prove his innocence in a second trial, and rarer that a convicted murderer is exonerated by a juror, yet that's exactly what happened in the case of North Carolina death row inmate Alan Gell.

Gell was a victim of a blatant miscarriage of justice and some very bad lawyering. He was convicted of murdering a man named Allen Ray Jenkins. The problem with the conviction was that Gell had a very good alibi at the time of Jenkins' death – he was in jail for another crime. Yet that didn't stop an investigator from manufacturing evidence that was used to convict Gell.

When did the Murder Occur?

The miscarriage of justice started on April 14, 1995, when the decomposing body of Allen Ray Jenkins was found in his home in Aulander, N.C. Jenkins' chest had been blown away with a shotgun. Jenkins was a very sleazy character who regularly lured teenaged girls to his home and traded alcohol to them for sex. Jenkins also reportedly liked to dress up in women's underwear.

Gell was arrested because two of the girls Jenkins liked to party with named him as a suspect. Gell claimed that he didn't know Jenkins and had never been to his house. The police arrested Gell, even though he had no motive for the crime.

The story developed by police and prosecutors was that Gell had killed Jenkins on April 3. Gell had to kill Jenkins on April 3 because he was out of the state for the next two days and in jail for car theft for several days afterwards. April 3 was the last day he could have killed Jenkins. The whole case would rest on the timing of the murder.

The problem with the prosecution's story was that 17 people reported seeing Jenkins alive after April 2. At least one person, a neighbor, had seen Jenkins as late as April 8 when Gell was in jail for car theft.

The Bureau of Investigation Lies on the Stand

The big problem was that none of those people were called to the stand at Gell's murder trial in 1998. Investigators were definitely aware of those witnesses, and one of them was even mentioned in the medical examiner's report on Jenkins' death. Yet that information was never provided to Gell's defense attorneys, a clear violation of the rules in a murder trial.

If that wasn't bad enough, there was evidence that a so-called investigator for the North Carolina Bureau of Investigation deliberately ignored clues and suppressed evidence. Dwight Ransome collected the statements from the 17 witnesses and completely ignored them because their testimonies hurt his case. Worse, he and two prosecutors from the state Attorney General's office deliberately withheld the evidence from Gell's lawyers.

If that wasn't bad enough, Ransome knew that the main witness against Gell, Crystal Morris, had been caught on tape saying she had made up a story for police. Ransome found this out by recording one of Crystal's phone conversations.

The prosecutors and Ransome might not have gotten away with it if Gell had an effective lawyer, but he did not. Gell had four court appointed lawyers in a three-year period, none of whom seriously investigated the case or challenged the prosecution's claims. In 1998, Gell was found guilty of first-degree murder and sentenced to death.

Saved by the Death Penalty?

Ironically enough, being sentenced to death was probably what got Alan Gell a second trial. North Carolina law requires that the state appoint two attorneys to examine every aspect of a death penalty case after conviction. The idea is to create an airtight case that will hold up on appeal.

These lawyers, Mary Pollard and James P. Cooney III, were able to go over everything, including all law enforcement files. Pollard quickly realized that the prosecution had not established the time of Jenkins' death. Instead, they simply stated he was killed during April 3-8. That was critical because Gell had sound alibis for the days after April 3.

The attorneys called in forensic experts to establish the time of death, something that Ransome should have done, but did not. They also began going through the files and soon unearthed mounds of evidence that disproved the state's story. Among other things, they found a tape of Crystal Morris's admission that her testimony was rehearsed, as well as the statements from the 17 people who saw Jenkins after April 3.

Second Trial and Vindication

Pollard and Cooney filed a motion for a second trial, which was granted. The second trial, held in 2004 in the same courthouse as the first trial, had a very different outcome.

In the second trial, all the evidence that had not been admitted at the first trial was presented by the defense. The prosecution didn't have a leg to stand on, and the jury delivered a not guilty verdict after two hours of deliberation. Alan Gell walked out of the courthouse a free man. Everybody in the courtroom, including David Ray, the murder victim's son, was convinced of Gell's innocence.

Taxpayers Foot the Bill

The first thing that Alan Gell did after the second trial was to file a lawsuit against the State Bureau of Investigation and Dwight Ransome. The Bureau settled the case with Gell in 2009 for $3.9 million after *The Charlotte News & Observer* newspaper published an article that reported the Bureau's own lawyers believed it would lose a civil case. *The News & Observer* also reported that the state spent $731,062 on a legal defense against Gell's suit.

Gell may not have enjoyed his victory much, because at that time, he was serving a five-year prison sentence for having sex with a 15-year-old girl. *The News & Observer* also reported that Ransome was still working with the Bureau and drawing a five-figure salary.

One thing is certain: Alan Gell is set for life under the terms of his settlement. He will receive $7,857.28 a month from an annuity for the rest of life. The real losers in this farce were the taxpayers of North Carolina.

Bibliography

Neff, Joseph. "A witness, a tangled web." 9 December 2002. deathpenaltyinfo.com. Charlotte News & Observer Feature Article. 26 June 2013.

—. "Evidence points to innocence." 11 December 2002. deathpenaltyinfo.org. Charlotte News & Observer Feature Article. 26 June 2013.

—. "Gell defense left in dark." 10 December 2002. deathpenaltyinfo.org. Charlotte News & Observer Feature Article. 26 June 2013.

—. "Gell investigator ignored blatant clues." 4 October 2009. newsobserver.com. Charlotte News & Observer Newspaper Article. 26 June 2013.

—. "State pays $3.9 million for wrongful conviction." 2 October 2009. newsobserver.com. Charlotte News & Observer Newspaper Story. 26 June 2013.

—. "Who killed Allen Ray Jenkins?" 8 December 2002. deathpenaltyinfo.org. Charlotte News & Observer Feature Article. 26 June 2013.

Wikipedia. "Alan Gell." n.d. en.wikipedia.org. Online Encyclopedia Article. 26 June 2013.

Anthony Porter

Few people have been as lucky or as unlucky as Anthony Porter. He once came within 50 hours of being executed for a crime that he did not commit. Yet he was freed because of unusual circumstances that revealed serious problems with his trial and conviction.

Like a lot of wrongfully convicted people, Porter ended up in prison because he was poor and had a bad lawyer. His case was a textbook example of almost everything that was wrong with the American justice system. Porter didn't get a good defense, and because he was poor and African-American, his case became a political problem for influential politicians in Illinois.

The Crime and the Wrong Man

The crime was a shocking and senseless one that was typical of its place and time: the South Side of Chicago in 1982. Two African-American teenagers, Jerry Hillard and Marilyn Green, were gunned down apparently in cold blood at a public swimming pool. The shooter had stolen some cash and jewelry from Green.

Police almost immediately fingered Anthony Porter as a suspect because he was a known gang member and had a criminal record for robbery. When he heard police were looking for him, he walked into the local police station to protest his innocence. Porter thought he could set the record straight; instead, he was quickly arrested.

Anthony Porter was an almost perfect fall guy for the crime because he had a criminal record and he was not very intelligent. Psychological testing later showed that Porter had an IQ of 51, which indicated that he could be considered mentally retarded. Police charged Porter with the crime even though there was no evidence linking him to it. Nor did they have a very good witness to the case.

A Questionable Witness and Another Suspect

Police were able to produce a very questionable witness named William Taylor. Taylor, who had been in the area, first denied he saw anything, but after 17 hours of interrogation at the police station, Taylor changed his story to say that he had seen Porter shoot Green and Hillard.

Police also learned there were two other suspects: a local drug dealer named Alstory Simon and his girlfriend, Inez Jackson, who had been seen with the victims. Ofra Green, Marilyn Green's mother, was the witness who had seen them together. Detectives never investigated her claims and allowed Simon to move to Milwaukee. Instead, they bought Simon's and Jackson's story that they were not in the park.

The Lazy Lawyer

The real villain in Anthony Porter's story is not the police but his defense lawyer, Akim Gursel. The Porters, who were poor, hired Gursel and paid him $3,000. Gursel took the case but stopped working on it when the Porters couldn't come up with the rest of the $10,000 he was charging. Instead, the lazy lawyer pretended to go through the motions.

Gursel didn't hire a private investigator to check out Taylor's testimony or Mrs. Green's story. He simply showed up in court and called three witnesses. Nor did he challenge the prosecution's case. Some witnesses even claimed that Gursel fell asleep in court.

Since Gursel made no defense, the jury found Porter guilty and sentencing began. Gursel waived Porter's right to a jury verdict so the judge would decide whether to sentence him to death or not. The judge sentenced Porter to death because he had been convicted of robbery and probation violations in 1979 and 1980. Porter had also threatened a man named Earl Lewis in an argument over a dog.

50 Hours Away from Execution

Antony Porter would spend over a decade on death row and at one point come within 50 hours of execution. Several appeals were filed on Porter's behalf, one of which made it all the way to the U.S. Supreme Court, which rejected it.

Attorneys for Porter argued that Gursel had failed to call witnesses whose testimony would have identified other suspects and cast doubt on William Taylor's claims. These witnesses included a woman named Joyce Haywood, who claimed to have seen Alstory Simon and Inez Jackson with Green and Hillard. Another witness, Ricky Young, claimed that Simon had a motive to kill Hillard. Young alleged that Hillard had been dealing drugs for Simon and skimming part of the profits for himself. The Supreme Court rejected this argument because Gursel hadn't mentioned these witnesses in an earlier appeal.

Porter's luck changed when a Chicago attorney named Daniel Sanders took his case on a pro bono basis. Sanders had Porter's IQ tested and learned it was 51, which meant Porter could be legally considered mentally retarded or intellectually disabled. When the Illinois Supreme Court learned of this, it granted a stay of execution just 50 hours shy of Porter's appointment with the death penalty.

Saved by Journalism Students

Porter's next stroke of luck reads like a script from a Hollywood movie. A journalism professor named David Protess was teaching a course in Media and Capital Punishment at Northwestern University. The course curriculum included investigation of actual death penalty cases.

Four of Protess's students chose Porter's case and started reviewing the case documents. The documents raised so many questions that the students visited the crime scene: a pool at Chicago's Washington Park. They held their own reenactment and concluded that William Taylor couldn't have seen the murder from the place he had been sitting on, which was a nearby bleacher.

The students hired a private investigator named Paul Ciolino, who tracked down William Taylor. Taylor admitted that he had never seen Anthony Porter shoot anybody and claimed police had used intimidation and threats to get him to change his story. Taylor even signed an affidavit to this effect.

Confession via TV News

The students were so intrigued that six of them continued with the investigation even though the class had ended. One of them, Erica LaBorgne, went to death row and talked to Porter. Porter told them to look for Inez Jackson, whom he claimed could finger Alstory Simon for the murders.

The students eventually located Inez Jackson, who was living in Milwaukee under the name Margaret Simon, and her nephew, Walter Jackson. Both told them the same story: that Alstory Simon had shot Green and Hillard in a fight over drug money. Margaret Simon even let them videotape her confession, which was played on CBS's national news broadcast.

Paul Ciolino then went to Milwaukee to confront Alstory Simon. Simon denied everything until Ciolino turned on the CBS news, which was showing Margaret's confession. Simon then claimed that he had shot Hillard and Green in self-defense during an argument.

Vindication after Two Decades

The Cook County State's Attorney (district attorney) filed a motion for Porter's release as soon as he heard of Simon's confession. Porter was released, and on September 7, 1999, Alstory Simon pleaded guilty to Green and Hillard's murders and received a sentence of 37 years in prison.

Porter's case raised serious questions about the death penalty in Illinois. These led Illinois Governor George Ryan to commute all 167 death sentences in the state in 2003. In a press conference announcing the move, Ryan mentioned the Porter case and said it convinced him that capital punishment in the state needed to be reformed. In 2011 Illinois became one of the first states in the United States to abolish the death penalty.

Bibliography

Capital Punishment in Context. "The Case of Anthony Porter." n.d. capitalpunishmentincontext.org. Website Designed as a Resource for College Courses. 25 June 2013.

Wikipedia. "Anthony Porter." n.d. en.wikipedia.org. Online Encyclopedia Entry. 25 June 2013.

Brian Banks: From Wrongful Conviction to the NFL

Many wrongfully accused people receive vindication and get back their freedom, but few get to extract a measure of justice from their accuser. Brian Banks did that and more. He not only got his reputation back, but he also got to make the person who ruined his life with false accusations pay. Then he had the satisfaction of getting a second shot at his dream of playing professional football.

In 2002, Brian Banks seemed to be living out the dream that millions of American boys wished they had. At age 16, he had already been offered a full scholarship to the University of Southern California (USC), one of America's top football factories, and he hadn't even finished high school. Banks seemed destined for gridiron glory and possibly a chance to play in the National Football League, yet one small indiscretion led him down a very different path and nearly destroyed his life.

Teenage Indiscretion leads to a Nightmare

Brian Banks' nightmare began with an everyday teenaged behavior. He and a girl named Wanetta Gibson decided to make out in a stairwell at Long Beach Poly High School. When the tryst was over, Gibson turned against Banks and accused the linebacker of rape.

It isn't clear why Gibson accused Banks of rape. Perhaps he spurned her advances, or maybe she just didn't like him. Yet the results of the charges were horrendous, and Banks was arrested and charged.

Even though there was no physical evidence of rape, Banks' attorney recommended that he plead guilty to the charges. Banks took the deal because the lawyer had insisted that he would be sentenced to 40 years in prison at trial. That meant there was no trial and Gibson was never cross-examined. Her allegations were allowed to stand.

End of the Dream

Banks lost his scholarship and his reputation. Instead of playing linebacker at USC, he ended up serving five years in prison. When he got out, he had no education, no job, no career, and no chance of getting into the NFL. Instead, he had to live with his mother and wear an ankle bracelet because he was now a convicted sex offender.

The situation was intolerable because Banks knew he was innocent, and worse, he knew that Wanetta Gibson was profiting from his pain in a big way. She had sued the Long Beach Unified School District and received a $750,000 settlement. Other reports claim the settlement might have been as high as $1.5 million.

Gibson had not only destroyed a man's life with her false accusations, but she had also figured out a way to make money from it. Worst of all, there was little Brian Banks could do about it until Gibson did something very stupid.

Stupidity on Facebook

Banks' luck turned in 2011 when he checked his Facebook page and found a new friend he didn't want. Wanetta Gibson sent Banks a request to become his new friend. Gibson added a message that indicated she wanted to forgive Banks.

Banks wasn't in a very forgiving mood. He decided it was time to fight back against the woman who had destroyed his life. He and his brother hired a private investigator who tricked Gibson into coming to his office.

At the office, Gibson made yet another stupid move. She said, "No, he did not rape me." The accuser didn't realize that Banks and his PI were videotaping everything she said.

For good measure the PI asked, "Did he kidnap you?" Gibson replied, "No."

Banks doesn't know why Gibson reached out to him or confessed. He thinks she might have wanted to renew their relationship. How she expected Banks to forgive her after five years in prison and the loss of his career was something she never explained. Obviously, Gibson must at the very least be incredible naive if she really thought a man whose life she had destroyed would want to date her.

Exoneration and Professional Football

Brian Banks had no money for an attorney, so he contacted the California Innocence Project, a charity that fights for the wrongly convicted. The Innocence Project took the unusual step of taking his case because of the evidence. The project's attorneys had little trouble getting the charges against Banks' conviction thrown out.

Soon after his exoneration, Banks got a second chance to live his dream. Several NFL teams, including the Washington Redskins, the Kansas City Chiefs, the Miami Dolphins, and the Seattle Seahawks called him in for tryouts for the 2012 season. He didn't make the cut then, but on April 3, 2013, Banks signed with the Atlanta Falcons.

Banks got some more satisfaction from a lawsuit he filed against Wanetta Gibson. On June 14, 2013, a Los Angeles County Court ordered Gibson to pay Banks $1.5 million in damages and $1.1 million in legal fees. Gibson may not be able to pay Banks because she has other legal and money troubles.

Less than a day after she lost her case to Banks, another court ordered Gibson to pay the Long Beach Unified School District $2.6 million. The school district sued Gibson when it learned that Gibson's claims were fraudulent. It wanted its money back from her.

Brian Banks not only got to live his dream, but unlike most wrongfully accused people, he got to see his accuser suffer the consequences of her actions.

Bibliography

Associated Press "Falcons sign Brian Banks." 3 April 2013. espn.go.com. Wire Service News Article. 29 June 2013.

Deutsch, Linda. "Brian Banks, CA Football Player Exonerated of Rape Charges After 5 Years in Prison." 24 May 2012. huffingtonpost.com. Associated Press News Article. 29 June 2013.

Hanzus, Dan. "Falcons' Brian Banks: I ate myself alive with negativity." 25 June 2013. nfl.com. NFL News Feature. 29 June 2013.

Kandel, Jason. "Woman Who Falsely Accused Brian Banks of Rape Ordered to Pay $2.6M." 15 June 2013. nbclosangeles.com. News Article. 29 June 2013.

Reilly, Rick. "Some NFL dreams never die." 30 May 2012. espn.go.com. ESPN Feature Article. 29 June 2013.

Smith, Michael David. "Brian Banks' Accuser ordered to pay back lawsuit settlement." 16 June 2013. profootballtalk.nbcsports.com. NBC News Blog. 29 June 2013.

Clarence Brandley

The legal battles of some wrongly accused individuals never seem to end. Take the case of Clarence Brandley. He's still fighting the state of Texas for restitution 33 years after being convicted of a murder he did not commit.

To add insult to injury, authorities attempted to collect unpaid child support from Brandley, who wasn't able to make the payments because he was on death row for a crime that he didn't commit. Since then, Brandley has been locked with the state in a legal conflict that doesn't seem to end.

Murder and Race in a Small Town

Clarence Brandley's nightmare began in 1980 when the body of Cheryl Dee Fergeson, a 16-year-old volleyball player, was found in the auditorium of a high school in Conroe, Texas. The girl had been raped and murdered.

The main suspects were the high school's five janitors. Charges of racism began flying soon after when police and prosecutors singled out Brandley, the only African-American working at the school. Brandley was arrested and charged with rape and murder because he was the only janitor who couldn't provide an alibi, not because there was any evidence.

Tried Twice for the Same Case

Brandley's first trial ended in a hung jury when one juror refused to find him guilty. That juror later complained that he had received thousands of threatening phone calls and racist threats because of his refusal to convict.

Brandley was tried again under even more questionable circumstances. Before his second trial, the physical evidence in the trial, including semen and hair samples from the victim, vanished from the courthouse. The evidence reportedly included a pubic hair that looked as if it belonged to a white man. It also included photographs that showed Brandley was not wearing a belt that prosecutors claimed was the murder weapon.

Instead, the only evidence introduced at the second trial was questionable testimony from the other janitors at the high school. The second jury convicted Brandley and sentenced him to death. What happened next was so dramatic that it was later made into a TV movie.

Dramatic Reprieve

Just days before his scheduled execution in 1986, Clarence Brandley was spared by a theatrical series of events. Brandley's defense attorneys were able to get two of the janitors who had testified to go on videotape and give a different account of events.

One of them, John Henry Sessum, stated that he saw two other janitors, Gary Acreman and James Dexter Robinson, who were both white, drag Fergeson into the bathroom. Acreman made a videotaped confession of his own in which he fingered Sessum as the real killer. The case soon became more confused when Acreman, probably realizing that he could end up facing the death penalty, recanted the statements.

Incredibly, Texas Attorney General Jim Mattox then claimed that an investigation by his office proved Brandley was guilty. Interestingly enough, the investigation was based partially on lie detector tests, which are inadmissible as evidence in American courts.

Prosecutors Lose at Last

Mattox's efforts failed to convince Special State District Judge Perry Pickett, who heard testimony about the case and recommended that Brandley be given a new trial.

Pickett's recommendation was based on testimony from a Texas Ranger investigator. The investigator noted that a bloodstain on Fergeson's clothing was matched to blood type A. Brandley didn't have that type of blood, but Robinson and Acreman did. The investigator also admitted that no effort had been made to compare the missing pubic hair to Acreman and Robinson.

It took 14 months for the Texas Court of Appeals to rule, but it eventually agreed with Pickett and recommended a new trial. The prosecution appealed to the U.S. Supreme Court, which refused to hear the appeal. When the Supreme Court denied the appeal, the prosecution dropped all charges, which enabled Brandley to walk out of death row as a free man.

No Justice for Anybody

Even though prosecutors showed they had no case against Brandley, they kept claiming that they had convicted the right man. None of the officials responsible for the travesty of justice were ever disciplined.

If that wasn't bad enough, the likely suspects, Robinson and Acremen, were never charged with the rape and murder of Cheryl Dee Fergeson. Whoever destroyed the physical evidence probably doomed any chance of convicting them.

Clarence Brandley is still fighting for compensation, but hasn't got it because of a legal technicality. Since he was never declared innocent, Brandley is not eligible for restitution. Brandley has had to fight another legal battle with state agencies that tried to collect unpaid child support payments from him. The legal nightmare is dragging on and on and nobody received any justice.

Interestingly enough, Clarence Brandley is no longer a janitor. He is now a Baptist minister who works with anti-death penalty groups in Texas.

Bibliography

Applebome, Peter. "The Truth is Also on Trial in a Texas Death Row Case." 4 October 1987. nytimes.com. New York Times Feature Article. 1 July 2013.

Connelly, Richard. "Clarence Brandley: Ex-Death Row Inmate Still Fighting for Restitution." 18 May 2011. blogs.houstonpress.com. Houston Press Newspaper Article. 1 July 2013.

Wikipedia. "Clarence Brandley." n.d. en.wikipedia.org. Online Encyclopedia Entry. 1 July 2013.

Earl Washington Jr.

Earl Washington Jr. was the victim of two acts of injustice. First he was sentenced to death for a murder he didn't commit. Then he was placed in prison for life for the same crime even though DNA evidence proving his innocence was available. To add to the injustice, evidence had been suppressed for blatantly political reasons.

Washington was typical of wrongfully accused individuals; he was poor, he was black, and he was intellectually challenged. When he was arrested and convicted for the murder of 19-year-old Rebecca Williams in 1984, Washington had an IQ of 69. There was also evidence that Washington was mentally retarded because of brain damage he had suffered as a boy.

Five Different Confessions

The tragedy began in 1982 when Rebecca Williams was raped and stabbed to death in front of her two young children in her own home in rural Virginia. The crime was exceptionally brutal; the assailant stabbed Williams 38 times.

Washington was arrested and questioned during the investigation of the crime. Washington's disability made him submissive to authority figures and eager to please. He apparently didn't understand what was happening to him or what police officers were asking. Police were interested in Washington because he apparently knew her family.

Psychologists later determined that Washington would try to cover up his disability by deferring to others and answering yes to their questions. He was easily manipulated into making a false confession.

It was later determined that Washington confessed to five different crimes, but police threw four of those confessions out for lack of evidence. They accepted the confession for Rebecca Williams' murder.

Saved by a Stroke of Luck

Earl Washington was found guilty of the murder of Rebecca Williams in 1984. The prosecution's case was based on questionable forensic evidence and Washington's confession. The young man was sent to Virginia's death row, where execution was scheduled for September 1985.

Washington avoided execution only because another death-row inmate, Joseph Giarrantano, told death penalty opponent Marie Downs that a mentally disabled man was facing execution. Downs told a lawyer who took Washington's case to a New York law firm that picked it up on a pro bono (charity) basis. The lawyers filed a writ of habeas corpus that halted the execution. The New York attorneys then appealed the case to the federal courts.

The case dragged on until 1993 when the U.S. Court of Appeals for the Fourth Circuit ruled that Washington had been denied the right to effective counsel. The court's justices felt this way because the defense failed to challenge forensic evidence.

Condemned by Politics

By 1993 DNA analysis was available, so Washington's lawyers decided to see if the new technique could help their client. A DNA test found that semen found on Williams' body did not match Washington's.

Despite this evidence, Washington was condemned to several more years in prison because of politics. The new evidence was barred from use in court because of a Virginia law that gave defendants 21 days after a conviction to present new exhibits. Instead, the evidence was taken to Virginia governor Douglas Wilder. Based on the evidence, Wilder commuted Washington's sentence to life in prison but did not pardon him.

Wilder did not say why he didn't pardon Washington, but politics probably played a role in the decision. Wilder, a Democrat, was considering a presidential run, and he wanted to be seen as tough on crime. Another Democrat, Bill Clinton, had just won the presidency partially on his record of allowing executions. Wilder, an African American, may have also been concerned that white voters would have turned against him if he was seen as favoring a black defendant.

To be fair to Wilder, Washington had other criminal convictions for burglary and assault in his record. There were also some doubts about the accuracy of the DNA testing, which might have given Wilder reasons for concern. At the time of the commutation, Wilder told reporters that he believed Washington's confession.

Spending Another Seven Years in Prison

Washington would have to spend another seven years in prison because of Wilder's refusal to act. His lawyers kept working on his behalf and once again turned to technology for help.

By 2000 a newer, more accurate DNA test was available, and Washington's attorneys had it used on the evidence from the Williams crime scene. Once again the test confirmed that the semen present didn't belong to Washington. The test wasn't the only new thing working in Washington's favor; there was a new governor in office in Richmond.

Governor Jim Gilmore was a white Republican who wasn't running for president, so he had no political reasons not to pardon Washington. Gilmore announced the results of the new STR DNA tests and granted Washington an unconditional pardon on October 2, 2000. Washington walked out of prison on February 12, 2001 but had to accept parole because of other unrelated charges he had been convicted on.

Washington's case proves two things about wrongfully convicted people. New technology such as DNA testing can sometimes clear them, but politics still plays an important role in justice. At the end of the day, politicians will still put their careers ahead of justice.

Bibliography

Green, Frank. "Richmond Times-Dispatch." 18 April 2000. truthjustice.org. Richmond Times-Dispatch Newspaper Article. 25 June 2013.

PBS Frontline. "Four Cases." 2000. pbs.org. PBS Frontline Website Feature. 25 June 2013.

The Innocence Project. "Know the Cases Earl Washington." n.d. innocenceproject. Innocence Project Website Feature. 25 June 2013.

The Justice Project. "Earl Washington Jr." n.d. victimsofthestate.org. Website Feature. 25 June 2013.

Juan Roberto Melendez-Colon

Many wrongfully convicted individuals are the victims of jailhouse snitches, criminals that try to better their own situations by informing on other inmates. Not surprisingly, a lot of jailhouse snitches are liars, but their false testimony can send innocent people to jail and even death row.

A typical victim of such a snitch was Juan Roberto Melendez-Colon, or "Puerto Rican Johnny". Melendez-Colon was an ex-convict and migrant farm worker who could barely speak English when he was arrested for murdering a man he claims he never met in 1983.

The man was Delbert Baker, or "Mr. Del", the owner of a hair salon in Florida. Baker was found dead at his business, and police were unable to find any evidence linking anybody to the crime.

Fingered by a Snitch

Melendez-Colon was linked to the crime by a man named Daniel Luna Falcon, a longtime snitch who had an extensive criminal record. Falcon reportedly had a grudge against Melendez-Colon and even threatened to kill the suspect at one time. The grudge may have stemmed from a dispute between Melendez-Colon and Falcon's parents.

Police put out a warrant for Melendez-Colon's arrest, which enabled FBI agents to track him down and arrest him in Pennsylvania. He was extradited to Florida, where Falcon served as the principal witness against him.

The prosecution presented no physical evidence linking Melendez-Colon to Baker at the trial. Instead, they relied upon Falcon's testimony that Melendez-Colon had killed Baker, even though Melendez had an alibi that he claimed was backed up by four witnesses. Melendez said he was with a woman named Dorothy Riviera.

Unable to Defend Himself

Melendez-Colon was unable to defend himself because he could barely speak English and couldn't read or write the language. He had grown up in Puerto Rico, even though he had been born in Brooklyn. He admitted that nobody tried to interrupt what he was saying to officers and his lawyer.

There was another even worse miscarriage of justice involved in the case. Another man had actually confessed to Baker's murder on tape and Melendez-Colon's attorney had the tape. Astonishingly, the tape was never entered into evidence at the trial.

In the tape, a man named Vernon James said he and another man had murdered Baker. There was also a statement from a witness named Terry Barber, who had seen James and another man at Baker's hair salon on the night of the murder. Another jailhouse snitch came forward and said that Vernon James had confessed the murder to him. That snitch claimed James and Baker had been lovers who had fallen out.

On Death Row for 16 Years

In a cruel twist of fate, Melendez-Colon languished on death row for 16 years and had his appeal denied by the courts three times. Neither Melendez-Colon nor the courts were aware that James had confessed to the crimes or that a tape of the confession was available. Since James had died in the meantime, his confession was admissible evidence.

Fortunately, luck was on Melendez-Colon's side in 2000. One of his attorneys stumbled across Vernon James' confession, and with this evidence in hand, the lawyers were able to locate witnesses that corroborated the statement. The evidence convinced Justice Barbara Fleischer of Florida's Supreme Court that grounds for a new trial existed. She ordered a new trial in the case.

Instead of retrying Melendez-Colon, prosecutors simply dropped the case. They didn't bother bringing it back to trial because Falcon was dead and some of the witnesses from the first case had changed their testimony. Even though they didn't say it publicly, the prosecution admitted that they had no case.

Fighting for Justice

Juan Roberto Melendez-Colon walked out of prison in 2002 and into a very different life than what he had known. "Puerto Rican Johnny" not only now knew how to speak English; he spoke it well enough to become a public speaker and an outspoken critic of the death penalty.

Melendez-Colon now travels the world speaking against the death penalty and works with anti-capital punishment groups, such as Journey of Hope and the National Coalition against the Death Penalty. He has toured several countries, including Germany, to speak against the death penalty. The illiterate farm worker has become an activist and public speaker who now lives in Albuquerque, N.M., far from Florida.

The killers of Delbert Baker have never been brought to justice. Vernon James died without facing trial and his accomplice has never been caught or tried for his role in the killing. Not only did a jailhouse snitch condemn one innocent man to 16 years on death row, the snitch helped the real murderers get away scot fee.

Bibliography

Juan Melendez Tour. "Juan Melendez Tour 2007."
2007. juan-melendez-tour.de. German Language
Website. 25 June 2013.

Voices United for Justice. "Juan's Story." n.d.
voicesunited4justice.com. Website Feature. 25 June
2013.

Wikipedia. "Juan Roberto Melendez-Colon." n.d.
en.wikipedia.org. Online Encyclopedia Entry. 25 June
2013.

Kirk Bloodsworth Makes History

Kirk Bloodsworth made history in a way that he would have probably have liked to avoid. Bloodsworth was the first person cleared of murder charges through the use of DNA evidence in 1993. He became the first American who was freed by a new technology that has since cleared hundreds of innocent people all over the world.

The aptly named Bloodsworth's brush with history began with a brutal crime in 1984: the rape and murder of a nine-year-old girl named Dawn Hamilton outside of Baltimore. Police had no leads to the horror until they received a very questionable tip from an anonymous caller. The caller claimed Bloodsworth was with Hamilton on the day she was murdered.

Police arrested Bloodsworth based on that dubious statement. In March 1985, Bloodsworth was convicted based on some very shaky evidence. The evidence consisted of drawings made by a police sketch artist and a footprint that couldn't be matched to Bloodsworth's shoes.

Tried and Convicted Again

Bloodsworth was sentenced to death, but he appealed the sentence. Eventually the Maryland State Court of Appeals overturned Bloodsworth's first conviction after his lawyers proved that prosecutors had withheld evidence.

So Kirk Bloodsworth had to live the nightmare of being tried for a crime he didn't commit again. The second time around he was spared the death penalty but sentenced to life in prison for a crime he didn't commit. He seemed to be without hope, but science was coming to the rescue.

DNA to the Rescue

In an incredible coincidence, the science that would free Kirk Bloodsworth was invented the year that he was falsely accused of murder.

On Sept. 10, 1984, Alec Jeffreys, a researcher at the University of Leicester in England was looking at x-rays of DNA. Jeffreys made the incredible discovery that the DNA of every human being in the world was unique. That meant samples of blood, skin, hair, and other material from human bodies could be matched to a particular individual.

Jeffreys had invented the DNA profile, which is now routinely used to match evidence to suspects. This was far more accurate than earlier methods, such as matching blood types and footprints. Unfortunately for Bloodsworth, it would be years before such profiles were available to law enforcement.

Saved by Reading

Like many inmates, Kirk Bloodsworth had a lot of
spare time on his hands, so he spent a lot of time
reading. In 1992 Bloodsworth read a book that
described how British police had used Jeffreys'
method to catch a serial killer called Colin Pitchfork.

Bloodsworth realized that the DNA testing might help
him because police had the murder weapon used to
kill Dawn Hamilton: a bloody rock the sexual
predator had beaten the girl to death with. Police also
had the underwear the girl had been wearing, and the
underwear contained the rapist's semen.

Bloodsworth asked his lawyers to push for new
testing. At first they seemed to be out of luck because
cops thought the underwear had been thrown out.
Then in a weird twist, the underwear and the rock
turned up in a paper bag in a judge's chambers.

Saved by Science

Testing that was done at two different laboratories showed that there was no way Bloodsworth could have been the killer. His DNA did not match that taken from the semen on Dawn Hamilton's underwear. Bloodsworth was released from prison and even paid compensation.

Yet he was determined to find the real killer in order to get justice and prove that he was innocent. Bloodsworth started campaigning to get the DNA evidence checked against databases containing DNA samples from known criminals. Eventually Bloodsworth convinced investigators to conduct the test in 2003.

The test identified Dawn Hamilton's real killer as a convict that Bloodsworth had actually done time with. Kimberly Shay Ruffner had served a sentence for attempted murder in the same prison where Bloodsworth was held. The two men had actually met in the weight room and the prison mess hall on a daily basis for nearly five years.

Ruffner, a convicted sex offender, pleaded guilty to Hamilton's murder in 2004. He received a sentence of life without parole for the crime, which he is still serving. Bloodsworth was given a full pardon because of Ruffner's identification.

Changing the Way Crimes Are Investigated

Kirk Bloodsworth became a lobbyist and a crusader for innocent people. He even started lobbying Congress and helped get a law called the Innocent Protection Act passed. The act actually provided $15 million in federal funding for DNA testing under the Kirk Bloodsworth Post-Conviction Program. This gives states money to set up laboratories to test DNA.

Bloodsworth has not only helped to free large numbers of innocent suspects, he has helped many people avoid the nightmare he was trapped in by preventing false accusations. Bloodsworth has also helped save lives by enabling authorities to catch and lock up real predators so they couldn't kill and rape again.

Today Kirk Bloodsworth is continuing his crusade for justice. He even got the chance to meet Sir Alec Jeffreys. Jeffreys was knighted by Queen Elizabeth for discovering what is now known as DNA fingerprinting.

Bibliography

Marshall, Claire. "I was first death row inmate saved by DNA." 9 September 2009. news.bbc.co.uk. BBC News Feature Article. 1 July 2013.

The Innocence Project. "Kirk Bloodsworth." n.d. innocenceproject.org. Website Feature. 1 July 2013.

WBAL TV News. "Kirk Bloodsworth marks 20th year since exoneration." 28 June 2013. wbaltv.com. WBAL TV news article. 1 July 2013.

Leroy Orange

Leroy Orange was the victim of multiple injustices at the hands of the courts and law enforcement. Not only was Orange wrongfully accused of four murders, but he also claims that he was tortured by Chicago police. Orange also claims that the torture was used to extract a false confession that was the basis of the case against him. To top it off, Orange spent nearly 20 years on death row for crimes he did not commit.

Perhaps the worst aspect of Orange's case was the identity of the person who helped frame him by corroborating the false confession: his own half-brother, Leonard Kidd, who was apparently the one who had committed the murders that started the nightmare.

Torture on the South Side

Leroy Orange's nightmare began on Jan. 12, 1984 when the bodies of Renee Coleman, Ricardo Pedro, Michelle Jointer, and Coleman's 10-year-old son Tony were found in a burning apartment on Chicago's South Side. All four had been tied up and stabbed.

Police quickly found a suspect in Leonard Kidd, who was walking around wearing Pedro's watch. Cops took Kidd to the police station, where he almost immediately started trying to frame Orange. Kidd told detective that Orange and "two dudes with knives" had committed the crime. Kidd was already a suspect in a 1980 arson fire that had killed 10 children.

Orange was arrested and brought to the station. Once there, his treatment was like something in a third-world country. Orange claims he was beaten, suffocated, and subjected to classic electroshock torture techniques often used by Communist governments. After 12 hours of such abuse, Orange confessed to the murders. The torture was allegedly committed by a group of rogue cops with the sinister nickname "The Midnight Crew" that was allegedly led by a police commander named John Burge.

Kidd, who also claims to have been tortured, then led police to the knives, yet he kept up the story that Orange had committed the murders.

Conflict of Interest

Leroy Orange's nightmare was compounded by incompetent legal counsel and bungling in the courtroom. He and Kidd retained the same private attorney, Earl Washington. That was a clear conflict of interest, but Washington kept the case for three months before withdrawing as Kidd's lawyer.

Washington was facing three charges of incompetence from the Illinois state body that regulated attorneys at the time of Orange's trial. The attorney was so inept that *The Chicago Tribune* made him the centerpiece of a story about bad lawyers.

At Orange's trial, Kidd changed his story and confessed on the stand and under oath that he had committed the murder. Kidd said Orange had been at the murder scene, but left before he started killing. No other witnesses or evidence linking Orange to the killings were presented at the trial.

Despite the testimony and torture allegations that were raised at the trial, Orange was found guilty and sentenced to death. Kidd pleaded guilty to murder to avoid the death penalty, but that didn't work and Kidd was also sentenced to death. The death sentence was overturned, but Kidd remained on death row until 2003 for the 1980 crime.

19 Years on Death Row

Leroy Orange would spend 19 years on death row awaiting execution for a crime he didn't commit. His situation was made worse by the appeals he kept filing and the court's rejection of them.

The courts kept rejecting Orange's claims because there was no physical evidence to verify his allegations of torture. A doctor who examined Orange's story noted that his confession was consistent with the behavior of torture victims, who often make false claims to end the abuse.

Even though Orange's lawyers couldn't confirm the torture, they could verify the allegations against Washington. They claimed Washington had failed to do his job properly, which resulted in Orange's death sentence.

Pardon and Cash

Leroy Orange's case was eventually taken up by Northwestern University law professor Thomas F. Geraghty, who assigned a group of law students at the Bluhm Legal Clinic to look into Orange's case. The students concluded that Washington had failed to look into Orange's torture allegations and challenge the prosecution's case.

Geraghty and his students failed to impress the courts with their cases, but they did impress Illinois Gov. George H. Ryan, a critic of the death penalty who believed Orange's story enough to issue a full pardon. That enabled Leroy Orange to walk out of death row a free man. In a press conference announcing the pardon, Ryan blamed rogue cops for Orange's conviction.

Leroy Orange's first action after leaving prison was to sue the City of Chicago and Cook County. The city eventually settled a wrongful conviction lawsuit with Orange for $5.5 million. A few years later, the Cook County Board agreed to pay Orange $525,000 in five payments.

Neither the city nor the county admitted it had done anything wrong in Orange's case. The former police commander whom Orange blamed for the torture, John Burge, was found guilty of obstruction of justice in 2010 by a federal jury for lying about the torture in a civil case.

The man who actually committed the murders, Leonard Kidd, is serving life in prison. Kidd had his death sentence commuted in 2003 when Gov. Ryan commuted the sentences of all death row inmates in Illinois. The state of Illinois has since abolished the death penalty.

Leroy Orange now travels around the world and speaks about his case. Not surprisingly, Orange has become an outspoken critic of the death penalty and police brutality.

Bibliography

Bluhm Legal Clinic. "Leroy Orange." n.d.
law.northwestern.edu. Website Feature. 26 June 2013.

Conroy, John. "Tools of Torture." 3 February 2005.
chicagoreader. Chicago Reader Feature Article. 26
June 2013.

Dardick, Hal. "County pays $525,000 to former
Death Row Inmate in wrongful prosecution case." 2
May 2010. newsblogs.chicagotribune.com. Chicago
Tribune News Blog. 26 June 2013.

Death Penalty Information Center. "Innocence Cases:
1994-2003." n.d. deathpenaltyinfo.org. Website
Feature. 26 June 2013.

Parkin, Joan. "Meet the Death Row 10: Leonard
Kidd." December 2003. nodeathpenalty.org. Feature
Article. 26 June 2013.

Walberg, Matthew and William Lee. "Burge found
guilty." 28 June 2010. articles.chicagotribune.com.
Chicago Tribune News Brief. 26 June 2013.

Wilgoren, Jodi. "Citing Issue of Fairness, Governor Clears Out Death Row in Illinois." 12 January 2003. nytimes.com. New York Times News Article. 26 June 2013.

Lucia de Berk

Most cases of wrongful convictions involve a real crime, usually a murder. What is usually fake is the testimony or accusations, and in some cases, the evidence. In the case of Dutch nurse Lucia de Berk, even the murders never occurred. De Berk spent six years in prison for a killing spree that never occurred.

She ended up falsely accused and wrongfully convicted for being in the wrong place at the wrong time. A series of bizarre coincidences and a set of very dodgy statistics turned Lucia de Berk into a suspect in the worst case of serial killing in Dutch history.

Statistics and Murder

Lucia de Berk was a licensed pediatric nurse who was working in three different hospitals in The Hague, Netherlands in 2000 and 2001. She came under suspicion when a number of patients in the wards she was covering died. One of the 14 deaths she was suspected in was of Haopei Li, a judge at the war crimes tribunal in The Hague and a citizen of China.

Investigators used statistics to make the claim that de Berk had poisoned the children with morphine. The basic theory was that the death rate in wards where de Berk had worked was higher than in normal wards. There were between nine and 14 suspicious deaths between 1997 and 2003 when she was arrested and charged with seven murders.

The problem with these claims was that there was no actual physical evidence linking de Berk to the crimes, nor were there any witnesses who had seen her poisoning the patients. The investigators and prosecutors tried to claim the statistics pointed to murder, but they could also indicate a tragic coincidence.

Convicted by Statistics

The prosecutors based their entire case on statistics that supposedly showed the odds of children and patients dying were 342 million to one. The problem was that some statisticians analyzed the numbers used and discovered that they told a different story.

Experts analyzed the mathematics used and determined that one of the experts, Henk Elffers, actually combined unrelated numbers in an attempt to get what he wanted. It should be noted that Elffers was a law professor, not a mathematician or a statistics expert.

The only physical evidence that prosecutors had was the drug dioxgen, which was found in the body of a baby that died on de Berk's watch. There was no evidence or testimony that indicated de Berk had administered the drug to the baby. Prosecutors also entered de Berk's diary as "evidence." De Berk was convicted on seven counts of murder and sentenced to life in prison based on nothing but statistics.

Saved by Statistics

Lucia de Berk was probably freed by an unlikely champion, Richard Gill, a professor of mathematical statistics. Gill, who was teaching at the University of Leiden, followed the case in the press and began questioning the numbers used.

Gill became so interested in the case that he began writing papers about it and carefully analyzing the data. What he discovered was rather disturbing – Gill determined that the numbers didn't add up. The statistics were based on a dossier assembled by the police, rather than actual hospital records. Gill even noted that one of the murders occurred when de Berk had not been in the hospital for three days.

He also calculated that that the actual odds of deaths in the hospital were one in 48, not one in 342 million. That meant the deaths were far more likely to be accidents, or of natural causes, rather than murders.

Cleared by the Numbers

Once he determined that the evidence used against de Berk was flawed, Gill launched a campaign to get her conviction overturned. He talked to the press and enlisted a number of celebrities, including other scientists, in his efforts. The crusade attracted press attention and the case was reopened.

The Posthumous II Commission, an organization that examines court cases in the Netherlands for errors, began an investigation of the de Berk case. The Commission eventually agreed with Gill's conclusion. Among other things, it noted that the prosecution and its experts had not compared the rate of deaths in the hospital wards at the times de Berk was there to the times when she was not present. The statisticians had not checked to see if death rates were the same when de Berk was not in the building.

The commission ruled that the case should be reopened and the Dutch Supreme Court agreed. The court overturned de Berk's conviction in October 2008. The nurse was freed from prison and a new trial was ordered. A new investigation into the deaths was held, and a number of them were found to be natural deaths.

Not Guilty by Reason of Statistics

In a second trial in April 2010, a court found that Lucia de Berk was not guilty of the murders. The prosecution was not able to make a case against her without the flawed statistical evidence.

The Dutch media reported that Lucia de Berk had received an undisclosed amount of money from the government of the Netherlands as compensation for her wrongful conviction and imprisonment. She continues to live and work in the Netherlands, but she cannot go back to nursing. An investigation revealed that she had lied about her grades in high school on her application for a nursing license, so the woman who been convicted by one set of false numbers was tripped up by another.

Bibliography

BBC News. "Dutch nurse 'killed' war crimes judge."
19 June 2002. murderpedia.org. BBC News Article
reprinted at Murderpedia.org. 27 June 2013.

Blanco, Juan Ignacio. "Lucia de Berk." n.d.
murderpedia.org. Online Encyclopedia Entry and
Other Materials. 27 June 2013.

DutchNews.nl. "Nurse Lucia de Berk not guilty of
murdering seven patients." 14 April 2010.
murderpedia.org. Wire Service News Article
Reprinted at Murderpedia.org. 27 June 2013.

Goldacre, Ben. "Lucia de Berk - a martyr to
stupidity." 9 April 2010. badscience.net. Guardian
Newspaper Column Published at Bad Science
Website. 27 June 2013.

Hawkes, Nigel. "Nigel Hawkes: Did statistics damn
Lucia de Berk?" 10 April 2010. independent.co.uk.
Independent Newspaper Column. 27 June 2013.

Osborn, Andrew. "Dutch nurse gets life for murdering four patients." 25 March 2003. murderpedia.org. Guardian Newspaper Article Reprinted at Murderpedia.org. 27 June 2013.

—. "Dutch nurse 'killed 13 by lethal injection." 18 September 2002. murderpedia.org. Guardian Newspaper Article Reprinted at Murderpedia.org. 27 June 2013.

Michael Roy Toney

The events surrounding the wrongful conviction and
exoneration of Michael Roy Toney are a real mystery.
The crime Toney was falsely accused of committing
was a bizarre bombing that seems ripped from the
pages of a paperback thriller. The reason Toney was
accused of the crime remains unclear. The mystery is
made even deeper by Toney's suspicious death in a
car accidently shortly after he walked away from
death row.

The Exploding Briefcase

The mystery surrounding Michael Roy Toney began with a bizarre tragedy that occurred to the Blount family of Lake Worth, Texas on Thanksgiving Day, 1985. After dinner, the man of the house, Joe Blount, drove three teenaged relatives to the convenience store while his wife Susan took a nap. At some point Susan was awakened by a knock on the door, but when she answered the door all she found was a briefcase which she brought inside, but didn't open.

When Joe Blount and the teenagers returned home, one of them, Angela, opened the briefcase. Angela didn't realize that the case contained a bomb with enough explosive force to destroy their mobile home. The bomb went off when she opened the case and killed five of the six people in the home. Only one member of the family, a 15-year-old son, survived the bombing.

Police were baffled by the explosion. They didn't know if the five people killed were the targets or victims of a tragic accident. The case remained open and unsolved, and there were no suspects until 1997.

The Jailhouse Snitch

Investigators finally caught a break in June 1997, when a jailhouse snitch named Charles (or "Jack") Ferris came forward. Ferris claimed that Toney had confessed to the bombing. Investigators were skeptical of Ferris' claims, but Toney's ex-wife, Kim Toney, wasn't. She looked into the incident and decided her husband was guilty. The ex-wife went to federal authorities, who later indicted Toney on six counts of murder.

The prosecution's case started to fall apart almost immediately because Ferris started denying the confession story. Instead, he now claimed that he and Toney had made up the bomb claims in order to get out of jail earlier.

Even though Ferris had recanted, another jailhouse snitch named Finis Blakenship came forward and claimed that Toney told him he had been paid $5,000 to kill the Blount family. Ferris, who was accused of child molestation, claimed that the bombing was a contract killing ordered by drug dealers; this story and testimony from Toney's ex-wife became the center of the prosecution's case.

The Trial and Death Row

Michael Roy Toney was convicted of six counts of murder and sentenced to death, based entirely on these questionable stories. No physical evidence connecting him to the crime and no motive was presented at the trial.

Toney claimed he hadn't heard of the murders until 1997, 12 years after they occurred, and he didn't even know where the crime scene, the Hilltop Mobile Home Park, was until trial. Toney also said that Kim had lied about the case on the stand. Among other things, he noted that she said he was driving a pickup truck at the time of the killings. Toney claimed he didn't buy a pickup truck until Dec. 13, 1985, over two weeks later.

There was also no connection between Toney and the victims. Prosecutors never established a motive or proved that Toney knew the Blount family. They did prove that Toney was in Lake Worth, Texas, near Fort Worth at the time of the explosion. There was another bigger problem with the prosecution's case. Fourteen pieces of evidence that contradicted the official story were deliberately withheld from the defense.

Death Row and Exoneration

Michael Toney ended up spending nearly 11 years on death row and waited as his case was appealed. Eventually, the appeals reached the Texas Court of Criminal Appeals, which had learned about the suppressed evidence. The court overturned Toney's conviction and sent the case back to courts in Tarrant County in 2009.

The Tarrant County District Attorney's office, which was accused of suppressing evidence, decided to excuse itself from the case. The local prosecutors wanted nothing to do with the matter, so they turned it over to the Texas State Attorney General's Office. The attorney general investigated and discovered that there wasn't enough evidence to make a case against Toney.

Toney was allowed to walk out of jail a free man in September 2009. He had to face other charges, including allegations he had a cellphone on death row in direct violation of prison regulations.

Mysterious Death and a Lingering Mystery

Michael Toney enjoyed his freedom for a little over a month. He died in a car accident on Oct. 3, 2009, and even though authorities ruled the death was an accident, people immediately began asking questions. There were rumors that he might have been killed to cover up the truth or murdered in revenge for the Blount killings. The Blount family's relatives even raised the possibility that Toney had faked his own death and disappeared.

The questions about Toney's death, the reasons for the prosecution, and the accusations that led to it remain unanswered. The mystery of the Blount family's tragic deaths remains unsolved.

Bibliography

Blanco, Juan Igancio. "Michael Roy Toney." n.d. murderpedia.org. Online encyclopedia entry and other materials. 27 June 2013.

Boggs, Clara A and Michael Roy Toney. "Michael R. Toney case account." n.d. murderpedia.org. Justice: Denied Magazine Feature Article Reprinted at Murderpedia.org. 27 June 2013.

Carlton, Jeff. "Former death row inmate freed after conviction overturned." 4 September 2009. murderpedia.org. Statesman Newspaper Article Reprinted at Murderpedia.org. 27 June 2013.

Lowe, Michael. "Crime News: Michael Toney Dies Within Weeks after being Freed From Texas Death Row, Are You Suspicious?" 7 October 2009. dallasjustice.com. Blog Entry. 27 June 2013.

Wikipedia. "Michael Roy Toney." n.d. en.wikipedia.org. Online Encyclopedia Entry. 27 June 2013.

Ray Krone

Being tried and convicted for a crime you didn't commit is a more common occurrence than most of us would like to admit. Being tried and convicted twice for a crime of which you are innocent is rare, but it happened to a man named Ray Krone. Not only was Krone tried and convicted twice for a crime of which he was wrongfully accused, but he was sentenced to death for it.

Krone's case was rather unusual for a wrongfully accused man because he didn't have a criminal record. Instead, Krone was a Postal Service employee who had served honorably in the U.S. Air Force. That makes his case all the more shocking and disturbing.

Krone ended up in prison and death row twice because he happened to be in the wrong place at the wrong time. He was accused of murder for drinking in the wrong bar.

Drinking in the Wrong Bar

Krone's nightmare began in December 1991, when he was drinking at the CBS Lounge in Phoenix. The body of a bartender named Kim Aconda was found in the men's room. Aconda had been stabbed to death sometime after the bar closed but not sexually assaulted.

Police arrested Krone because another bar patron told them he was going to help the victim close the tavern that night. Police used circumstantial evidence, including bite marks that matched a Styrofoam cup Krone had bit and the fact that blood in the men's room was type O positive, to make the case. That was Krone's blood type, but it was also the blood type of 42% of the population, including one other patron. It was also Kim Aconda's blood type. The forensics testing available to Phoenix police in 1991 didn't let them differentiate between blood types.

In 1992 Krone was convicted of first-degree murder and sentenced to death. The prosecution's case was based largely on questionable testimony about bite marks. Krone believes the jury bought the prosecution's story because he relied on a public defender rather than hiring his own attorney. The testimony about teeth got Krone the nickname the Snaggletooth Killer in the press because of the shape of his mouth.

Déjà vu All Over Again

The case against Krone was so shaky that he was able to win an appeal, but prosecutors again pressed charges against him. The prosecution was able to make the same case a second time.

Yet doubts had been raised even in the mind of the judge. The judge gave Krone a sentence of life imprisonment rather than the death penalty because the jury had serious doubts about the case against Krone.

Krone went back to prison, but this time there wouldn't be another successful appeal. He would have to wait 36 years to be eligible for parole. Instead, it was forensic science, which had sent him to prison, that would set Ray Krone free.

Set Free by DNA

When Ray Krone was first tried for murder in 1992, DNA testing was in its infancy. Police investigators had to rely on highly inaccurate measurements, such as blood types, rather than the much more accurate DNA when they tried to link individuals to a crime.

By 2002 DNA testing was commonplace and a proven method. Krone's cousin Jim Rix, a very wealthy man who owned a software company, had paid for the defense at the second trial. Rix decided to see if DNA testing could help his cousin and paid for testing.

The testers didn't find any of Krone's DNA, but they did find DNA belonging to a man named Kenneth Phillips, who lived in the area. Phillips was also a convicted child molester—whose DNA was on file in an FBI database.

One of Krone's attorneys, Alan Simpson, went to see Phillips, who was serving prison time for another crime. Phillips made a number of incriminating remarks. Krone was ordered set free shortly afterwards and returned to Pennsylvania, where his family lived.

Extreme Makeover

Ray Krone's case attracted publicity because he was the 100th death row inmate proven innocent since the U.S. death penalty was restored in the 1970s. Since his release, Krone has remade himself over as an anti-death penalty activist who has spoken all over the world.

Ray Krone also became a very wealthy man by settling a lawsuit against Maricopa County, Ariz., for $1.4 million and another suit against the City of Phoenix for $3 million. Krone used his money to finance his anti-death penalty crusade and buy a farm in his hometown of Dover, Penn.

In 2005 Krone attracted even more attention by appearing on the popular ABC TV show *Extreme Makeover*. The program paid to have Krone's teeth fixed and his face made handsome through plastic surgery. Krone's attorney told reporters that his makeover cost the TV network around $200,000.

Krone received an unusual honor on Feb. 20, 2006, when both houses of the Arizona State Legislature voted to apologize to Krone. The legislators gave Krone a standing ovation after the apology.

Ray Krone's story is one of the more unusual tales of wrongly convicted men. He was tried twice but eventually achieved a much higher level of justice than most people in the same situation. Kenneth Phillips was eventually convicted of the murder of Kim Aconda and sentenced to life in prison in the third murder trial held in her case.

Bibliography

CBC. "Ray Krone." n.d. cbc.ca. CBC Feature Article. 25 June 2013.

Krone, Ray. "Take It From One Who Knows: Death Penalty System Is Broken." n.d. ccadp.org. Commentary. 25 June 2013.

The Innocence Project. "Know the Cases: Ray Krone." n.d. innocenceproject.org. Website Feature. 25 June 2013.

Ron Williamson: The Innocent Man

Ron Williamson was a victim of tragic circumstances who became a celebrity and a rallying cry for opponents of the death penalty. He was an ordinary man who spent 12 years on death row for a crime he didn't commit.

Much of the interest in Williamson's case stemmed from his career in minor league baseball in the 1970s. A star athlete in high school with a batting record of .500, Williamson was a second-round draft pick of the Oakland Athletics in 1972. Williamson played two seasons of minor league ball in the Athletics' farm system before being sidelined by an injury. When he recovered, Williamson came back and pitched for two seasons in the New York Yankees' farm system, but a shoulder injury ended Williamson's career and dreams for good in 1977.

Baseball was Ron Williamson's life, and without it, he went down fast. He worked at menial jobs, became a drug addict and an alcoholic, and started suffering from mental illness. Williamson ended up living with his mother in Ada, Okla. and spending his time drinking.

Drinking at the Wrong Bar

Ron Williamson became a suspect in a brutal rape and murder because he drank at the wrong bar, the Coachlight Club in Ada. In December 1982, the citizens of Ada were shocked when Debra Sue Carter, a waitress at the club, was raped and strangled in her own apartment. The killer even desecrated her body by writing on it with ketchup.

Williamson and his drinking buddy, Dennis Fritz, were singled out as suspects because they were hanging out at the Coachlight Club on the last night Debra Sue was seen alive there. Investigators questioned Williamson, but couldn't find any evidence. He underwent two polygraph (lie detector) tests, which were inclusive and useless because polygraph results are not admissible as evidence in U.S. courts.

Williamson and Fritz were finally arrested for the case five years later when a jailhouse snitch came forward and fingered them. Williamson was serving time for writing bad checks when the snitch claimed he had confessed to Debra Sue Carter's murder.

Questionable Evidence Leads to Death Row

Ron Williamson and Dennis Fritz were tried separately. Williamson didn't receive much of a defense at his trial – his public defender failed to introduce a videotaped confession to Carter's murder by Ricky Joe Simmons. The defender also failed to call witnesses and raise the issue of Williamson's lack of mental competency to stand trial.

Not surprisingly, Williamson was convicted and sentenced to death. He was moved to death row and kept in an underground cell for months on end without fresh air or sunlight. Williamson later claimed that guards would taunt him over the intercom at night to keep him from sleeping.

At one point in 1994, Williamson was just five days away from execution when a public defender filed a writ of habeas corpus, pointing out the lousy defense at his trial. The federal 10th Circuit Court of Appeals agreed and granted the writ and later a motion for a new trial.

Saved by DNA

Ron Williamson was saved by DNA analysis, a technology that didn't exist when he had first been tried for the crime. Williamson's attorney, Mark Barrett, got permission to conduct a DNA analysis of the evidence from Debra Sue Carter's body. He also approached a group called the Innocent Project, which investigates claims of innocence for help.

The project tested semen discovered on Carter's body and found the DNA in it didn't match that of Williamson nor Fritz. Instead, it matched the DNA of a man named Glenn Gore, who had testified against Fritz and Williamson at both their trials. Not only had Williamson been convicted of a crime he didn't commit, but one of the witnesses against him was the real murderer. Gore's DNA was on file because he was doing time for another crime.

Authorities in Oklahoma had no choice but to exonerate and release both Williamson and Fritz. Glenn Gore was later convicted of Carter's murder and sentenced to death in 2003. Ironically enough, that conviction was later thrown out and Gore was retried in 2006. At his second trial, Gore was convicted of first-degree murder and sentenced to life in prison.

Celebrity and Death

The case made Williamson something of a celebrity. He and Fritz made headlines by suing the City of Ada and the State of Oklahoma and winning. The two won $500,000 from Ada and an undisclosed amount from the state in 2003.

Williamson didn't enjoy the money and the fame for very long. He died in a nursing home of cirrhosis of the liver and other complications from alcohol and drug abuse in 2004.

Nor did Williamson live to see his story on the bestseller lists. In 2006, attorney, novelist, and outspoken death penalty opponent John Grisham published a nonfiction book called *The Innocent Man: Murder and Injustice in a Small Town.* The book subsequently became a bestseller.

Despite the publicity, some residents of Ada still think Gore is innocent and Williamson and Fritz were guilty. The courts have disagreed; Glen Gore is still in prison for the murder of Debra Sue Carter.

Bibliography

Associated Press. "Gore Avoids Death Penalty in 2nd Trial." 26 June 2006. kxii.com. Wire Service News Article. 25 June 2013.

Cockerell, Penny. "2nd trial begins for man given death sentence." 7 June 2006. newsok.com. Oklahoma City Times Newspaper Article. 25 June 2013.

PBS Frontline. "Burden of Innocence Ron Williamson." n.d. pbs.org. Frontline News Feature. 25 June 2013.

The Innocence Project. "Know the Cases - Ron Williamson." n.d. innocenceproject.org. Website Feature. 24 June 2013.

Wikipedia. "Ron Williamson." n.d. en.wikipedia.org. Online Encyclopedia Entry. 25 June 2013.

Sean Hodgson

Wrongfully convicted individuals often have to wait a long time for justice and vindication. No one seemed to have waited longer than Englishman Sean Hodgson, who spent 27 years in Her Majesty's prison system for a rape and murder that he did not commit.

Hodgson had to wait 27 years until new technology in the form of DNA testing became available and enabled investigators to clear him. Hodgson's case is a frightening one because it shows just how mistaken police and the courts can be.

Hodgson's story had some strange twists, including the fact that he was ultimately cleared by a man who had been dead for over 20 years. New forensic technology enabled police to put claims made by a man who had been in the grave for decades to the test and free an innocent man.

Murder at the Pub

Hodgson's journey into justice began in 1979 when the half-naked body of Teresa De Simone was found in the back of her car outside a pub in Southampton, England. An examination indicated that De Simone had been raped and strangled. The attacker had also stolen her jewelry.

Police soon found a suspect in the form of a local petty criminal and sex offender named Sean Hodgson. Hodgson, who has been described as a congenital liar, soon confessed to the case. Hodgson was too skilled at lying for his own good; everybody believed his false confession, including the police and a jury, which sentenced him to life in prison in 1982.

The Other Suspect and the Clerical Error

The case became more complicated in 1988 when another criminal named David Lace confessed to the De Simone murder. Nobody was able to check out Lace's story because he killed himself soon after making the confession. Investigators had no way to verify or deny Lace and Hodgson's stories until 2009.

The story couldn't be verified because evidence collected at the murder scene was missing. Hodgson's attorneys first approached a government agency called the Forensic Science Service about DNA testing in 1998. The barristers were told that testing couldn't be done because the evidence had been lost. Yet it hadn't; the samples had apparently been misfiled and stored away in a warehouse.

In 2008 Hodgson decided to hire a new law firm. The new lawyers launched a search and uncovered the missing evidence. That meant DNA tests could be carried out to see whose story was correct. It also meant that Hodgson had spent ten years in prison because of a clerical error.

Dead Men Do Tell Tales

The key to Sean Hodgson's innocence turned out to be a man who had been dead for over 20 years. In August 2009 police exhumed the body of David Lace from a cemetery in Portsmouth, England. Even though Lace had been buried for decades, investigators were able to extract enough DNA to perform the tests.

The testing showed that Lace had been telling the truth and Hodgson had been lying. Samples of DNA from De Simone's body matched Lace, which meant he was the real murderer. It also meant that Sean Hodgson had spent most of his adult life in prison for a crime he did not commit. Hodgson was released from prison in 2009 after a court quashed his conviction.

Hodgson was also a very lucky man; if David Lace's body had been cremated, he would have had no way to verify his story. He was also lucky that the missing forensics evidence turned up after 30 years. Even the best modern forensics technology still needs a helping hand from fate to free the innocent.

A Brief Taste of Freedom

Sean Hodgson enjoyed a very brief taste of freedom. He died of emphysema in October 2012, just three years after walking out of prison.

Even though he wasn't in good health, Hodgson didn't stay out of trouble after leaving prison. In May 2011 Hodgson was placed on supervised parole after being charged with sexual assault. He had apparently had an affair with a mentally disabled woman.

Don't Lie to the Police

Hodgson's case has been described as one of the longest miscarriages of justice in British history. It attracted a lot of criticism because it was determined that Hodgson was mentally ill and suffered from what was described as a personality disorder.

The mental illness may have been why Hodgson was willing to lie to police and confess to a crime he had not committed. Fortunately for Sean Hodgson, DNA doesn't lie, even though suspects often do.

Bibliography

BBC News. "Sean Hodgson, wrongfully jailed for 1979 murder, dies." 27 October 2012. bbc.co.uk. BBC News Article. 28 June 2013.

Laville, Sandra. "Miscarriage of justice victim served 11 extra years due to 'lost' evidence." 18 March 2009. guardian.co.uk. Guardian Newspaper Article. 28 June 2013.

Topping, Alexandra. "Police exhume body of suspect in 1979 murder." 12 August 2009. guardian.co.uk. Guardian Newspaper Article. 28 June 2013.

The Central Park Five

New York City was a very dangerous place in 1989. On an average day in that year, the NYPD responded to reports of 255 robberies, 194 assaults, nine rapes, and five murders. Citizens were scared to death, and the city was deeply divided along lines of race and class.

It was in this climate that a savage crime shocked and further divided the city and became a symbol of an area. The nightmare began on April 19, 1989, when a vicious sexual predator named Matias Reyes attacked, savagely beat, and raped Trisha Meili, an investment banker who was jogging in Central Park and left her for dead. Meili was so badly beaten that she couldn't remember what happened to her.

Reyes' attack on Meili occurred on the same night that a gang of young rowdies was roaming around the park attacking joggers and bicyclists. The young hooligans were black and Latino, and most of the joggers and bicyclists were white. Police responded and rounded up five of the punks. There was no connection between Reyes and the rampaging teens.

In the Wrong Place at the Wrong Time

Like many wrongfully accused people, Kharey Wise, Steve Lopez, Antron McCray, Kevin Richardson, and Yuself Salaam were simply in the wrong place at the wrong time. They were accused because they were in the park that night and the police already had them in custody.

When Meili was found, the five were already at the Central Park police precinct. The real attacker, Reyes, was long gone by the time the investigation started. The teens, who were not represented by a lawyer, confessed and even reenacted the crime for them. Police also claimed that as many as 20 teenagers might have taken part in the attack.

What happened was a classic example of false confession when a person, often poor, uneducated, and sometimes mentally impaired, confesses to a crime he or she didn't commit. This often occurs because the individual doesn't know any better or is so scared of the police that he or she will say anything.

Police were under intense pressure to solve the crime because 1989 was an election year and crime was one of the top issues. Voters were angry about violence in the streets and wanted swift action. Police delivered and the NYPD's Chief Detective, Robert Colangelo, went on TV and said the perpetrators had been caught. Colangelo also used the term "wilding" to describe the incident.

Sentenced to the Max

Even though the prosecution's account of the attack was completely wrong, a jury was convinced. Three of the five, McCray, Santana, and Salaam, were convicted of rape in September, 1990 and sentenced to 20 years in prison, even though there was no evidence and no reliable witnesses. Instead, the prosecution's hyperbolic statements seemed to move the jury. The trial further divided the city as the African American press and some politicians cried racism.

Another of the five, Kevin Richardson, was convicted of attempted murder and rape, while Wise was convicted of sexual abuse and assault. The city had been riveted by the trial, which was characterized by sensational testimony. There was little the five's attorneys could do to challenge the charges because there was no physical evidence to challenge.

The five were, in the words of the tabloids, "sentenced to the max." The main element swaying the jury was their confessions, which had been videotaped and introduced as evidence. Since the confessions contradicted the young men's claims of innocence, they were statements against interest and admissible in court. Even though the confessions were false the jury believed them.

The Monster Confesses

The five went to prison and New York began to change. Mayor Giuliani came into office and the crime rate started to fall. The hysterical fears of urban decay and racial Armageddon receded into history. Then in 2002, like a nightmare from the past, the Central Park Jogger case came back to haunt the city again.

Ironically enough, it was the man responsible for the horror in the first place who revived it. Matias Reyes went on nationwide TV, the ABC Network's *Primtetime Thursday* news magazine, and confessed to the attack. Reyes said he had been in the park stalking victims when the attack occurred.

When he confessed, Reyes was serving a long sentence for stabbing a woman to death two months after the "wilding" incident. Reyes told TV viewers how he had attacked Meili, and he even said he had talked to a cop right after the attack. The real attacker had walked out of the park while police were busy interrogating the wrongfully accused. Worse, he was able to get away with rape and murder.

DNA tests soon verified Reyes' claims and embarrassed both the NYPD and the Manhattan District Attorney's office. Manhattan DA Robert Morgenthau dropped the charges, which effectively ended the criminal cases against the five. The five walked free, but their case still haunts New York City.

The Case that Won't Go Away

The five sued New York for $250 million in a case that's still winding its way through the courts 22 years after the wilding. Recent press reports indicate that no trial date has been set in the case 11 years after it was filed. The Central Park Jogger nightmare never seems to go away or to end, even though the violent era that spawned it has receded into history.

Bibliography

Associated Press. "NYC is pressed to settle Central Park jogger case." 6 April 2013. usatoday.com. Wire Service News Article. 30 June 2013.

Cantwell, Alice, Joseph McNamara and Maria Mooshil. "2 Guilty in Jog Case." 12 December 1990. nydailynews.com. New York Daily News Article. 30 June 2013.

Griffin, Annaliese. "The Climate: New York in 1989." 8 April 2013. nydailynews.com. New York Daily News Feature Story. 30 June 2013.

Marques, Stuart. "Park Marauders call it: 'Wilding'." 22 April 1989. nydailynews.com. New York Daily News Article. 30 June 2013.

McQuillan, Alice. "A Monster's Tale Gruesome details of jogger rapists' confession." 22 September 2002. nydailynews.com. New York Daily News Article. 30 June 2013.

Smith, Chris. "Central Park Revisited." n.d. nymag.com. New York Magazine Feature Article. 30 June 2013.

The West Memphis Three

There are many reasons for wrongful accusations and convictions, but the strangest has to be listening to heavy metal music and wearing black. Yet that's exactly what happened to three teenagers from West Memphis, Ark. in 1993. They were accused of a terrible crime and sent to prison because of their tastes in music and fashion.

The case against Damien Echols, Jason Baldwin, and Jessie Misskelley still generates vast amounts of controversy two decades later. Their supporters believe that they were the victims of a modern-day witch-hunt. Their critics think they were cold-blooded killers and Satanists that got away with three incredibly brutal murders.

Atrocity in Robin Hood Hills

The drama began on May 6, 1993 with a horrible discovery in Robin Hood Hills, a working class subdivision near West Memphis. The naked and severely mutilated bodies of three young boys were discovered in a shallow grave in the woods. Almost as soon as the bodies were discovered, rumors began circulating that Satanists were responsible for the murders of Chris Byers, Michael Moore, and Stevie Branch.

At the time, there was a nationwide hysteria about Satanism and popular conspiracy theories that Satanists were kidnapping, molesting, and murdering children. Some of the theories tried to link Satanism with certain kinds of music, especially heavy metal.

These allegations were ridiculous, but authorities apparently believed them. The West Memphis Police turned to Jerry Driver, a self-educated cult and occult expert who was also a local cop. Driver started investigating local teenagers he felt were involved in the occult, even though there was no evidence that a Satanist conspiracy existed.

A Modern Day Witch Hunt

Driver's investigation quickly deteriorated into a modern-day witch-hunt. He started investigating various individuals whom he thought were involved in the occult. They included Damien Echols, a high school dropout, and Jessie Misskelley Jr., a misfit who liked to listen to Metallica and had an interest in the Wicca religion.

Misskelley was eventually taken to the police station, where he confessed to the crime several times. The only evidence Driver had besides Misskelley's confession was claims by some local kids that another teen named Jason Baldwin had thrown the murder weapon in a lake. There was no physical evidence, although the supposed murder weapon was found.

Despite the questionable case, each of the three were put on trial separately. Misskelley's trial was particularly questionable because the jury foreman had prior knowledge of the case, including Misskelley's confession. That was a clear violation of the rules governing trial procedure. The jury should have been dismissed and replaced with somebody unaware of the case.

Witch Hunter on the Stand

Baldwin and Echols' trial featured another self-proclaimed witch hunter, Dr. Dale Griffis. He claimed to be an expert on "Satanic ritual abuse", but his PhD came from a diploma mill. Another problem was that there was no such thing as Satanic ritual abuse, the kidnapping and murder of children by devil worshippers. The FBI had investigated and discovered no evidence of such conspiracies.

Dr. Griffis testified that the crime scene bore all the signs of occultism – the boys were murdered on the night of a full moon and a pagan holiday. He claimed that the mutilations bore all the signs of Satanic sacrifices. Griffis also claimed falsely that the boys' ages (they were all eight) and the number of the boys killed were significant. It was later determined that there is no basis to these claims.

Griffis also claimed that Satanists had killed the boys in order to drink their blood. Griffis claims recall the old old myth of blood libel: the absurd belief that Jews and Satanists drink the blood of the dead. The idea of blood libel has been around centuries but no actual case of it has ever been proven. Griffis's bizarre story unfortunately went unchallenged. Worse, physical evidence that pointed to other victims, such as a shoeprint from the area where the boys were found, was ignored.

Worst of all, Jessie Misskelley Jr. and Jason Baldwin were sentenced to life in prison and Damien Echols was sentenced to death. The only reason Echols was sent to death row was that he was over 18 at the time.

Freed by Filmmakers

The unlikely saviors of the West Memphis Three were two filmmakers, Joe Berlinger and Bruce Sinofsky, who decided to make documentary about the case. Ironically enough, Berlinger and Sinofsky seem to have believed the accusations against the three. They thought they could make a sensational film about Satanism.

After interviewing the three in prison and talking to the people of West Memphis, the filmmakers came to a horrifying conclusion. They had uncovered a modern-day witch trial in which a young man had been sent to death row. The two produced a movie called *Paradise Lost: The Child Murders at Robin Hood Hills*, which was eventually shown on HBO.

The film put a spotlight on the case and attracted a number of celebrity supporters, including Eddie Vedder of Pearl Jam, Natalie Maines of the Dixie Chicks, Metallica (Jessie Misskelley's favorite band), movie star Johnny Depp, and movie director Sir Peter Jackson of *Lord of the Rings* fame. Jackson reportedly donated $10 million to Echol's defense.

Jackson assembled a team of forensics experts that examined the case and the crime scene. The experts discovered that the boys' bodies had really been mutilated by snapping turtles. The bodies had been dumped in a water-filled gulley where the turtles lived. They also found no sign of the three's DNA at the murder scene, but the investigators found a strand of hair that matched Terry Hobbs, Steven Branch's stepfather.

Natalie Maines then suggested that Hobbs was the real killer. Hobbs sued Maines, but lost and gave her attorneys a deposition that suggested he was the real killer.

Despite the Hobbs and Maines' dispute, it was the DNA evidence that proved crucial. Attorneys filed a Writ of Habeas Corpus, which was granted by the Arkansas Supreme Court in 2010. In 2011, the three entered into a plea deal that let them leave prison.

The Drama Continues

Despite all of the publicity and investigation, the murders of Chris Byers, Michael Moore, and Stevie Branch remain unsolved, and Terry Hobbs has never been charged with the deaths, although Hobbs' ex-wife, Pam Hicks (Steven Branch's mother), now alleges that Hobbs committed the crime. Some news stories indicate that three other men, L.G. Hollingsworth, Buddy Lucas, and David Jacoby, may have assisted Hobbs with the killings.

These allegations haven't been proven, but one thing is certain: the drama surrounding the West Memphis Three is far from over.

Bibliography

Daily Mail Reporter. "New possible suspects named in brutal 1993 West Memphis murders of three cub scouts - including one of the boy's stepfathers." 28 March 2013. dailymail.co.uk. Daily Mail Newspaper Article. 27 June 2013.

Huffington Post. "Pam Hicks, Mother of West Memphis Victim, Names New Suspects in Affidavit." 29 March 2013. huffingtonpost.com. Huffington Post News Feature. 27 June 2013.

Rich, Nathaniel. "The Nightmare of the West Memphis Three." 4 April 2013. nybooks.com. New York Review of Books Feature Article. 27 June 2013.

Steel, Fiona. "The West Memphis Three." n.d. trutv.com/library/crime. Online Encyclopedia Entry. 27 June 2013.

West Memphis Three Facts. "The Real Memphis Three." n.d. westmemphisthreefacts.com. Website. 28 June 2013.

Wikipedia. "West Memphis Three." n.d.
en.wikipedia.org. Online Encyclopedia Entry. 28 June
2013.